Frederick an
A Christn

Written by Ned Atlas

Cover illustration by Roisin Murray

First published December 2023

I would like to thank everyone who has supported this series and I can't I wait to share more of Frederick and Winston's adventures.

Chapter One

On Christmas Eve, the most heart-warming of nights, after all the children of Cobbles Town have gone to sleep and milk and cookies can be found in every house in town, a small trail can be found in the snow leading to a red barn. Tiny paw prints alongside bird footprints lead the way to the slightly open door overlooking the town below.

As the barn draws closer what could be described as music starts to fill the air, a fast-paced beat with singing to match is coming from inside the home of two unlikely friends.

Inside can be found a proud barn owl named Winston beating out a tune using a stick and an old pot as his closest friend Frederick the mouse dances back and forth as he sings his joyful heart out.

The remnants of a large cabbage lay strewn about the barn with hay covering the floor and improvised stockings made out of old potato bags hung from the wall.

Fredericks singing slowly starts to fade as the two begin to make their way over to their beds. "That was a fantastic Christmas Eve. Your drumming is getting better every day" says Fredrick. "You flatter me Frederick but truly your singing warms the heart" responds Winston as the two laugh together.

This is the first Christmas the two friends have spent together since meeting, and neither could be happier. Their new and improved barn was wonderful, filled with little nooks for Frederick to sleep and store his winter clothes in. Winston loved the ample space between the rafters allowing him to spread his wings in the morning before the two ventured out into the town.

They had both been determined to make this Christmas as special as they could, decorating the barn with holly from the nearby woods. Fashioning a home-made wreath from an old tea tray and spare greenery from the market. Even going so far as to find a small unwanted Christmas tree that wasn't bought by the townsfolk, but they loved it and managed to drag back it to the barn.

Frederick slept in a small hole in the corner filled with straw. A small pillow and blanket made from an old scarf kept him warm through the cold Winter nights. One day Winston had found a discarded woolly hat and used it to insulate Fredericks room to ensure his friend would always have a warm home to sleep in.

A long yawn escaped from Frederick as he was much more tired than he had expected. As the two of them walked closer to his bed Frederick began to yawn more and more until Winston picked his friend up and laid him down in bed, tucking him in under the blanket.

"Thank you. This was the best Christmas Eve I have ever had," said a rather sleepy Frederick. "You are very welcome" answered Winston before saying "Tomorrow will be even more exciting though." The two friends laughed before saying goodnight as Winston flew up into the rafters.

Winston slept in a comfortable box that Farmer John, the owner of the barn, had provided for him. He had never known someone to care so much about the animals living in his barn, at times it even seemed that the farmer maintained the barn just for their sake.

As Frederick fell fast asleep Winston snuggled up to think about how much his life had changed since meeting his friend. The adventures they had been on together and laughter they had shared. He knew he didn't need any Christmas present this year; he had received the greatest gift he could have asked for already.

And with that the pair fell asleep dreaming of snowmen and Christmas dinner. Neither of them expected how important they would become over the next few hours.

Chapter Two

One by one snowflakes begin to fall over the sleeping town. Dreams of presents and food fill every home as fires slowly dwindle through the night. Every soul in town was soundly asleep, not one aware of the visitor making his way towards the now snow-covered town.

If anyone had been awake then perhaps they would have seen an odd shadow moving through the sky. As the shadow drew closer to the outskirts of the town it began to descend towards the red barn atop the hill. However, it failed to slow down enough as it approached the barn.

With a clatter and a bang it collided with the trailer parked outside the barn door. Inside could be found a sleeping mouse and barn owl who were immediately awoken by the noise.

"Winston. Did you hear that?" whispered Frederick as he grabbed his small coat and scarf. "I did indeed my friend. We should see what it was but make sure to stay behind me, I'll keep you safe" answered Winston as he flew down in front of Frederick.

The pale white mouse quickly got dressed as the pair of them heard the noise of something shuffling around outside. Ever so slowly they crept towards the door, curious as to what was going on outside. Oddly enough the two of them didn't feel afraid, despite neither of them knowing why they felt whatever was outside meant them no harm, in fact they felt warmer as they approached the door.

When the pair were merely whiskers away from the door Winston turned to Frederick behind him and nodded his head to which the mouse smiled and readied himself behind his friend.

Gingerly Winston pushed the barn door open. At first they couldn't see anything out of the ordinary until they gave the trailer a closer inspection, it was at an unusual angle with what appeared to be a velvet sack stuck on top of it. As they approached, they could see the sack was being pulled at by something on the other side, but it was refusing to move.

"Excuse me, is someone there?" called out Winston more puzzled than he expected to be by the sight. The sack stopped moving as the sound of hooves nervously clopping the ground could be heard coming from behind the trailer. "You don't need to be afraid, we would just like to help you" says Frederick as he moves to stand next to his friend.

Suddenly a small black nose emerges from behind the trailer, it sniffs the air three times before being followed by what appears to be the head of a small deer. Deep, kind brown eyes stare back at Frederick and Winston. Small antlers can be seen atop the animal's head sprinkled with the falling snow.

"I'm so sorry I didn't mean to wake anyone up", says the deer clearly nervous as it walks out into the open. Frederick can't quite believe his eyes, at first he believed it to be a regular deer but upon closer inspection he can see the fur is much too thick and dark to be a deer from the nearby woods. Excitement fills his voice as he splutters out "My goodness, are you a reindeer?".

"Now, now Frederick, we should introduce ourselves first before asking questions. I am Winston the barn owl and this here mouse is my good friend Frederick. What's your name?" said Winston as calmly as ever as he extended a wing to the stranger in a show of friendship.

The deer shuffled on the spot as it stared back at the duo before mustering the courage to say "My name is Reddy and yes, I am a reindeer. I did not mean to wake you up I just haven't quite gotten the hang of flying yet."

A few seconds of silence fill the air as Frederick and Winston stare back with mouths open. Not only is the new arrival a reindeer but he just said he can fly. Naturally Winston was the first to regain his composure before saying "You can fly, but you don't have any wings" all the while Frederick continues to stare amazed at what he has heard.

"It is true that I don't have wings but none of Santa's reindeer do. He shares part of his magic with us so we can fly, that's how the older ones such as my father are able to pull his sled. But I'm much too young for that since I still can't land properly".

Frederick simply stood there astounded by what he had heard as Winston's eyes widened further then they had ever been before. Eventually he squeaked up and said "You are one of Santa's reindeer, that's incredible.

But then why are you here on your own?".

Reddy shuffled around on the spot clearly nervous about the subject. Winston noticed how uncomfortable Reddy was becoming so he decided to try and calm the situation "My apologies we're simply so astounded that we forgot out manners, we mean you no harm, in fact if you tell us what's going on then perhaps, we can help you".

Reddy's face lit up at the offer of help "Thank you, oh thank you so much, it's such an important task, I would truly appreciate the help. You see this sack fell off Santa's sleigh as he was taking off and it is meant for the people of this town. If you could help me deliver the presents, I would be so very grateful" exclaimed the reindeer as he smiled at the thought of the duo's generosity.

Frederick needed no time to consider as he turned to Winston, giddy with joy before saying "We would be more than happy to help".

Chapter Three

Time passed as Reddy explained how he had seen the sack fall off the sleigh just as Santa was taking off from the North Pole. He had tried to catch up to him but was unable to fly fast enough, so he decided to try and deliver the presents himself to ensure the townsfolk weren't left out of Christmas. He was just leaving farmer John's house when he slipped on the roof and dropped the sack onto the trailer thus meeting our friendly pair.

Fortunately, Frederick and Winston knew most people in the town from the time they spent in the market and could direct Reddy to where each present needed to go. And so, the newly formed trio set out to deliver the first present to Paul the butcher who lived nestled at the bottom of the hill in a small stone cottage.

Reddy couldn't quite fly anymore since he had had such a tiring trip from the North Pole, so he trotted along as Winston flew overhead directing the small deer down the hill as Frederick held onto his friend's talons. Soon the three of them were outside the back window to the house facing an unexpected development, how would they get in.

"What does Santa usually do?" asked Frederick. "Well, he is magic after all, I'm sure he has plenty of ways to deliver presents" answered Reddy as he looked around for an idea. "May I look at the present in question" inquired Winston. As Reddy pulled the small present from the sack Winston lit up with an idea, the present was small and thin, if he could open the letter box on the front door then Frederick could place it under the tree.

He explained his idea to the group which was met with resounding support. The plan was simple, Winston would hold open the letter box as Reddy pushed the present through. Once it was inside Frederick would jump off Reddy through the open letter box and push the present along the floor into the living room and under the tree.

Frederick couldn't hide that he was a little nervous about the plan but knew that his friend trusted him. And so they began, Winston flew up to the letter box, grabbing it with both talons before pulling it up, Reddy held the present in his mouth before dropping it through the open letter box as Frederick climbed up on to his new friend and prepared to jump. Just as he reached the tip of Reddy's nose he stopped, nervous of what could happen, what if he fell or got lost in the house.

"There's no need to fret, my friend. I will be with you every step of the way" reassured Winston. Frederick felt his courage start to return as

Reddy chimed in to say "I wish I could be as brave as you are right now Frederick. Thank you so much for helping me like this".

With a full heart and a long leap, Frederick made it through the letter box and began climbing down the door. He had always been an incredible climber, so he naturally made his way down the door. Despite living in Cobbles Town for most of his life he had never been inside one the townsfolks homes before, it was quite a shock. The place was covered in decorations of all shapes and sizes, lights and colours dazzled his eyes as he made his way through to the living room where he was met with the most incredible sight. A tree nearly as tall the ceiling covered in tinsel, baubles, lights and decorations hung from every branch with a handful of brightly wrapped boxes underneath. He paused to take it all in before remembering the task at hand as he pushed the present neatly in-between two other boxes before one last look as he turned to leave.

He scampered up the door and out through the letter box once more before recalling everything he had seen in great detail to his friends. How he wished they could have seen it with him. After reciting his story, the trio set off to deliver the next present.

This box, addressed to Ava the baker, was larger than the previous one, too large for Frederick to push so they would have to find a different way to deliver this one.

Ava's house was located right next to the market square where during the day there had been celebrations that filled the town with the sound of music as people danced in the snow. Footprints leading in every direction were slowly being covered up by the falling snowflakes. The night was growing colder but they couldn't stop yet.

As they reached Ava's house Winston spotted a small plastic hole in the bottom of the door, he recognised it as the door meant for the houses cat. "Frederick, I would recommend you stay outside this time and let me deliver the present, why don't you sit on Reddy's back and warm yourself up" said Winston as he lifted Frederick off the ground.

It was true that Frederick was growing cold despite wrapping up as best he could, but he knew the real reason why his friend wanted to go instead. "Okay but come back soon" said Frederick as he sunk into Reddy's warm fur coat.

Reddy laid the present down in front of the door before leaning in to whisper to Winston "Are you sure about this". "Have no fear my good reindeer, I will be back before you even know I'm gone" and with that

Winston pushed the present through the small door and followed through.

Once inside the house he lifted his head up and was greeted by the most incredible sight, the house was nearly a perfect match to Fredericks story. Bright lights and candles lit the hallway as decorations hung from every possible surface. The smell of mince pies filled the air. He stood still for a moment soaking it all in before remembering the task at hand.

Ever so slowly he pushed the present through the hallway. In front of him stood three doors, one directly to his left, one to his right and one further along on the right. He decided to try the door on the left first. Gently pushing the door open revealed a room with much human furniture and what appeared to be a large black window in the centre but no tree.

Undeterred he closed the door and decided to try the opposite door. As he drew closer, he could see the door was slightly open with thin rays of light peeking through. He rested his wing against the heavy door and pushed It open revealing the source of the light to be a dazzling Christmas tree in the far corner of the room.

This one however did not match Fredericks description. It was rather tame with the same style of baubles hanging from each branch growing slightly bigger the lower they went.

Still it was a beautiful sight for the barn owl who had never been so close to a fully decorated Christmas tree before.

Once he regained his focus he returned to push the present into the room. Slowly but surely he made his way to the centre of the room when he suddenly heard a shuffling noise come from behind him. His turned around to see a bright orange and white cat sitting a few feet away from him simply staring at him with a curious look on his face.

The cat didn't say anything as the two continued to look at each other. Eventually Winston broke the tension by standing up straight and saying

"My deepest apologies for intruding on your sleep. The package that you see behind me is intended for Ava, as soon as I deliver it, I will be on my way". And yet the cat said nothing as it continued to stare back at Winston.

Winston was becoming nervous; he had never communicated with any of the cats in town outside of a short hello as he flew by. Suddenly the cat stretched out its right paw then its left as it let out a rather long yawn before saying "You must be that strange owl that lives in the barn atop of the hill with the pale mouse".

Winston was shocked, the cat knew him and knew of Frederick. "Yes that would be me, but would you mind telling me how you know of my friend and I" asked Winston. "That's simple" replied the cat "Every animal in town knows of you two, how your barn burnt down and the journey you went on. Only for you to return to find a brand-new barn waiting for you. Why the story of an owl becoming friends with a mouse was bound to spread. We heard it all from a crow a few months ago".

It must have been the crow they met in the woods on their way to the city, thought Winston. "But then why have you never come to see us" asked Winston. "We were afraid of scaring you away again. You two are what we might call an inspiration to the animals of this town. For years we cats had been afraid of the dogs in town whilst the birds were afraid of us. But when we heard about your friendship it made many of us wonder why we were afraid of each other at all. Slowly we became friends with the dogs and birds around town. The two of you are always up on the hill in your barn so it must have been hard for you to notice." The cat finished its story before rolling over and stretching.

Winston was amazed, had they truly inspired the animals of Cobbles Town to put aside their differences. This was incredible, truly something amazing and yet he hadn't known about it. The cat walked forward and extended a paw to Winston, he extended his wing in return. "My name is Whiskers, but you can call me

Whisk for short," said the cat. "I'm Winston, a pleasure to meet you Whisk.

Whisk helped Winston to place the present under the tree as Winston recalled his story about Reddy and the presents for the town. Whisk wanted to help however he could and asked if he could come along to the next house.

As the two were about to leave the house Winston asked his new friend to wait a few minutes as he explained this new development to Frederick and Reddy. He stepped outside and told his friends the news, Frederick was astounded by the news, amazed that their adventure had caused such a change in the town.

After a few minutes Winston went back inside to retrieve Whisk. As the pair stepped outside Reddy took one step back clearly still surprised by the dramatic change in the cat's nature. However not a word was needed between the mouse and the cat, they simply extended their paws and greeted each other, proud of this momentous occasion.

Chapter Four

The next present in need of delivery was intended for Hernan the postman's son. Seeing as the present was rather large and quite heavy it was left in the magical sack until the group reached the postman's home nestled in the middle of a quiet street with his van parked outside.

However, it seemed delivering this present would prove harder than anticipated, it was too large to fit through the letter box and there was no opening in sight. The trio seemed dismayed until Whisk pointed out that he was friends with the dog that lived here, a young lurcher named Biscuit.

Whisk jumped up onto the windowsill and knocked on the class three times, seconds later a commotion could be heard from inside the house before a bright white face appeared in the window. Whisk gestured to the door and instinctually Biscuit knew what he meant.

Moments later Biscuit was opening the door, surprised by the interesting group outside. "My, my what a surprise, an owl, a mouse and a reindeer have come to visit" said Biscuit as she spun around on the spot with joy. Unable to contain her amazement she ran up to Reddy and began sniffing him. "You smell like gingerbread and magic, it's nice to meet you" said Biscuit as she sat down in front of Reddy.

Reddy smiled back but couldn't find the courage to answer the overly excited dog. As Biscuit turned to face Frederick and Winston, Winston bowed his head as he said "It's always a pleasure to meet new friends, but sadly we don't have the luxury of time. We need to deliver more presents after this one and we would truly appreciate your help in getting this present inside".

Biscuit appeared confused before looking at Reddy, "Excuse me but if you're a reindeer why don't you fly to the roof and drop the present down the chimney?" as if in unison all members of the group began to look at Reddy and wonder why they had not asked the same question.

Reddy seemed to shrink on the spot as he began to stutter out an answer "I'm sorry but I can't fly very well yet, especially in front of others". The little reindeer looked so very sad as none of the group seemed to know what to say. The silence was broken by Frederick stepping forward and patting Reddy on his nose.

"No need to fret Reddy, you're amongst friends now. You can fly whenever you want. For now, let's focus on getting this present inside the house, we're going to need your strength to help push it under the tree". Reddy seemed nervous at the idea of going into the house, but Fredericks kind words and the smiles of his friends reassured him.

The largest present yet was pulled from the sack, nearly the size of Reddy, it barely fit through the door frame. All of the group lined up behind it and pushed with all their strength, even little Frederick joined in. As they crossed into the open hallway Reddy stopped, this was the first time he had ever been inside a person's house. It was so much smaller than he expected, nothing like the large stable he lived in at the North Pole.

He began to wonder what might happen if the people who lived here woke up and found them, what would Santa say if he was caught away from the Pole. His thoughts continued until Winston rested a wing on his back, patting him numerous times as Reddy calmed down. "Would you like to know something interesting; I think your amazing. You came all the way from the North Pole just to help save Christmas for our little town. I am certain that when you get back to the Pole Santa will see you as a hero. I know you're nervous but there's no need to be. You've already achieved so much, anything else is just icing on the cake, so to speak".

Reddy had never heard such kindness before, this bird he only met tonight was being so kind to him. Not just a bird though, a friend. With renewed strength he pushed the box once more and the group managed to bring it into the living room. One final push as Reddy gathered his strength against the side of the present as it moved towards the tree. Once it was in place, he turned around to find the rest of the group still standing in the living room doorway smiling back at him.

He was surprised until Frederick stepped forward and said, "We just wanted to show you that even though we aren't able to do what you can, we were right here with you the whole time". Reddy could feel tears starting to drop from his eyes as he realised he had found the Christmas present he had always wanted. He clicked his hooves together with joy as little sparkles started to dance beneath him. Glitter and gold moved in waves around his horns, suddenly he kicked off the ground and was flouting in the air. "Thank you" he said full of joy.

None of the group could quite believe it, a true flying reindeer was in front of them. Biscuit began wagging her tail in amazement and Whisk's jaw dropped open from surprise. Frederick and Winston simply stood there filled with pride for their new friend.

Reddy floated back down to the ground before leading the way back outside. "I can never thank you enough my friends," said the blushing reindeer. "I should be able to deliver all the presents much faster now. But I would love it if you would come with me". Frederick hopped on Reddy's back as Winston readied himself to fly alongside just before Whisk said "Biscuit and I should probably go home; we need to sleep before Christmas morning. It has been wonderful meeting you Reddy, if you ever come this way again do say hello", Biscuit spun around on the spot and waved farewell to the young reindeer and his friends before they took off into the sky.

Frederick couldn't quite believe his eyes; he had been flying before with Winston, but this was something else. Reddy moved as if he was running on the air, not a single wasted movement as he danced through the night sky holding the sack full of presents in his mouth.

Winston had always loved flying, but to do it with a friend was entirely new to him. An experience he was loving as he flew around and over Reddy, watching the little reindeer enjoy flying once more. Soon the trio descended on to a nearby rooftop where Reddy began rummaging through the sack. "Will putting it through the chimney really work" asked Frederick. "Oh yes" answered Reddy "Santa has been doing it this way for a very long time just in case anyone was still awake inside. The present slides down the chimney and finds its way under the tree. It's all a part of the magic of Santa".

And with that the trio all helped to lift the present down the chimney, certainly a much faster way than what they had been doing before.

In no time at all every house in town had received its present and Reddy was heading back to the barn where they first met. It had been an amazing night for them all, meeting new friends and the revelation of how the town had changed. Frederick could hardly believe he was now friends with a cat and a dog, as well as also being friends with a flying reindeer.

Reddy softly landed in front of the barns large red doors near the old trailer where they had first met, the empty sack hanging over his back. Once again, he looked sad as he knew he had to leave. "I hope we can meet again next Christmas" squeaked Frederick as he started to shiver from the cold. Winston put his wing around him to warm him up as Reddy smiled back. "Me too" said the little reindeer before clicking his hooves together and taking off into the night sky.

The two friends watched as Reddy flew off into the night sky. Quietly they turned around and walked back into the barn they called home. "What an incredible night that was Winston" said Frederick half yawning. "It certainly was" answered Winston as he laid Frederick down into his bed once more. The two of them said goodnight as they went to sleep dreaming of Christmas morning.

Chapter five

Christmas morning in Cobbles Town is always special. Families open presents together before playing in the snow. People gather in the market square singing carols and warming themselves by the open fire. It is certainly the happiest of days. But in a red barn, atop a hill, a barn owl and a mouse lay fast asleep, tired from the exciting night they had had.

No one in the town below knew that all their presents had actually been delivered by this unlikely pair, with help from a little reindeer and some new friends. Slowly Winston began to wake from his slumber, at nearly midday this was far later than he would usually sleep in. He knew that farmer John had gone to visit his family in town but would have probably left some food out for the two of them.

He flew down from his perch and poked at his friend attempting to wake him up. Frederick tossed and turned but eventually woke up with a long yawn. The two said good morning and wished each other a very Merry Christmas before making their way outside.

What greeted them was beyond their imagination. There in the snow sat a bright red sleigh with reindeer gathered around. A large man in a red and white coat with a brilliantly white beard and rosy cheeks stood beside it holding a small sack in his right hand. All around the barn stood every cat, dog, bird and animal from the town. The moment they saw Frederick and Winston emerge from the barn the crowd erupted in cheers shouting, "Merry Christmas".

Frederick and Winston were speechless until Reddy suddenly emerge from behind the man and said, "My friends, when I returned to the North Pole I told Santa all about what had happened and he said he just had to thank you in person".

The brightly dressed man walked forward, sack in hand. He knelt down in front of the pair. His eyes showed how kind-hearted he was as he looked the bird and mouse up and down. As he spoke his deep soothing voice filled the air "Now Reddy here tells me you helped him deliver all the presents for this town. And that you have inspired all the animals to become friends. You two truly hold the spirit of Christmas in your hearts. Please accept these gifts from me to you".

Santa reached into his sack and pulled out a bright red and white scarf, hat and mittens before handing them to Frederick. "These clothes have a little bit of magic in them, they'll keep you warm no matter the weather". "Thank you, Santa. Thank you so much" said Frederick as he lovingly took his new clothes. "And for you,

dear owl, I have something special.
For you are a deeply kind soul, so kind
I would trust you with this bell.
Should you ever need to visit me
simply ring the bell three times and
one of my reindeer will collect you".

Winston nearly teared up, Santa
trusted him so much that he would
give him something of such great
value. He accepted it with absolute
pride thanking Santa numerous times.

And with that the entire group began
to cheer. Before long a party began as
Frederick and Winston talked with
everyone as the reindeer danced
above. Cats and dogs sang Christmas
tunes as best they could as the birds
made a perfect chorus. Santa handed

out treats to all as the barn was filled with Christmas cheer. Food was shared all around as every animal in attendance swore up and down this was the best Christmas they had ever had.

In time the party began to slow as the guests made their way home full of food and cheer. Santa prepared the sleigh for the trip back to the North Pole as Frederick and Winston had one last goodbye with Reddy. "I asked my father if I could come and visit you both next year and he said yes" exclaimed Reddy happier than he had ever been.

"We can't wait," said Frederick. And with that the reindeer flew off into the sky as Santa waved goodbye. Winston could have sworn he saw the faintest of red light glowing from the reindeer at the front of the sleigh, but perhaps it was just his imagination. They watched as the sleigh disappeared into the clouds as snow fell all around them.

They stood outside the barn for some time simply taking it all in, eventually the silence was broken by Frederick saying "Winston, I'm so glad we came home" "Me too Frederick. Merry Christmas" "Merry Christmas to you too".

The End

Merry Christmas to everyone.

Printed in Great Britain
by Amazon